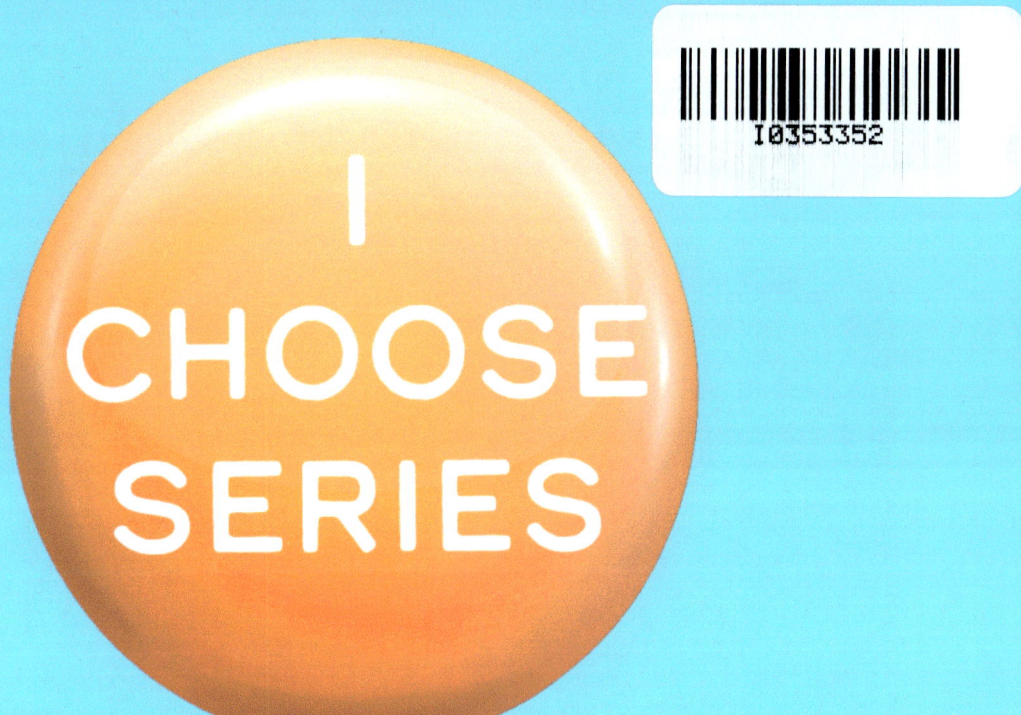

SEL CURRICULUM
by Elizabeth Estrada

Social, Emotional Learning • Worksheets • Activities

I Choose to Calm My Anger | I Choose to Calm My Anxiety | I Choose Kindness | I Choose to Try Again | I Choose to Reduce, Reuse, and Recycle | I Choose Happy

Shop all the I Choose products on toybookstore.com

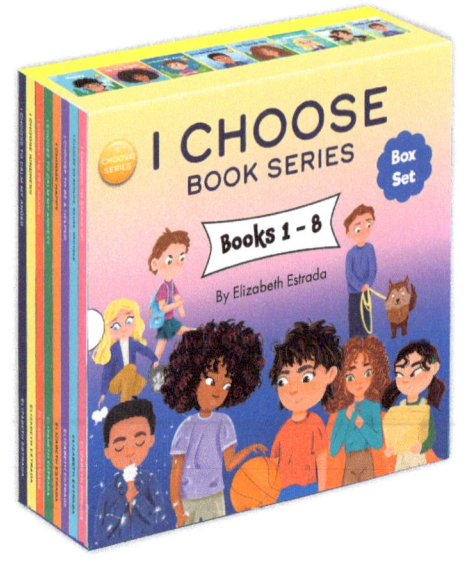
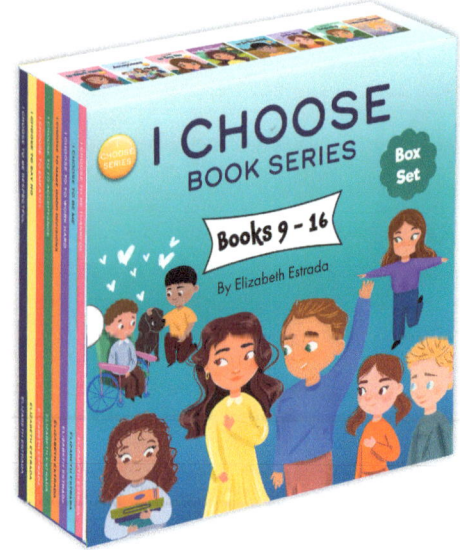

IT IS ILLEGAL TO POST THIS DOCUMENT ONLINE

The material enclosed is copyrighted. You do not have resell rights or giveaway rights to the material provided herein. Only customers that have purchased this material are authorized to view it. If you think you may have an illegally distributed copy of this material, please contact us immediately. Please email elizabethestradainfo@gmail.com to report any illegal distribution.

Copyright © Ninja Life Hacks and Elizabeth Estrada Inc. All rights reserved.

No part of this publication may be reproduced or transmitted in any form or by any means, electronic or mechanical, including photocopying or information storage and retrieval systems. It is illegal to copy this material and publish it on another web site, social media page, forum, etc. even if you include the copyright notice. Images copyright Elizabeth Estrada.

LEGAL NOTICES

While all attempts have been made to verify information provided in this publication, neither the author nor the publisher assumes any responsibility for errors, omissions or contrary interpretation of the subject matter herein. The publisher wants to stress that the information contained herein may be subject to varying state and/or local laws or regulations. All users are advised to retain competent counsel to determine what state and/or local laws or regulations may apply to the user's particular operation. The purchaser or reader of this publication assumes responsibility for the use of these materials and information. Adherence to all applicable laws and regulations, federal, state and local, governing professional licensing, operation practices, and all other aspects of operation in the US or any other jurisdiction is the sole responsibility of the purchaser or reader. The publisher and author assume no responsibility or liability whatsoever on the behalf of any purchaser or reader of these materials. Any perceived slights of specific people or organizations is unintentional. The author and publisher of this document and their employers make no warranty of any kind regarding the content of this document, including, but not limited to, any implied warranties of merchantability, or fitness for any particular purpose. The author and publisher of this document and their employers are not liable or responsible to any person or entity for any errors contained in this document, or for any special, incidental, or consequential damage caused or alleged to be caused directly or indirectly by the information contained in this document.

CONSULT YOUR PHYSICIAN

The techniques, ideas, and suggestions in this document are not intended as a substitute for proper medical advice! Consult your physician or health care professional before performing any exercise or exercise technique. Any application of the techniques, ideas, and suggestions in this document is at the reader's sole discretion and risk.

You can:
Use this resource for your personal use
Use this item (and make copies) for your classroom of up to 30 students
Use this item on google classroom and/or share with your students (you can not share on publicly searchable websites)

You can't:
Redistribute or use this resource for any commercial purposes
Modify or edit this document or its graphics and use in any way (including within free resources or sale resources)
Share or forward to other people who are outside of your home or classroom
Share on websites that are publicly searchable or upload to any social media networks such as Facebook.

All rights reserved. Permission granted to use resource as stated above. The reproduction of this product is strictly prohibited. Placing it on the internet in any form is strictly prohibited. Doing so is a violation of the DMCA.

I Choose to Calm My Anger
Lesson Plans

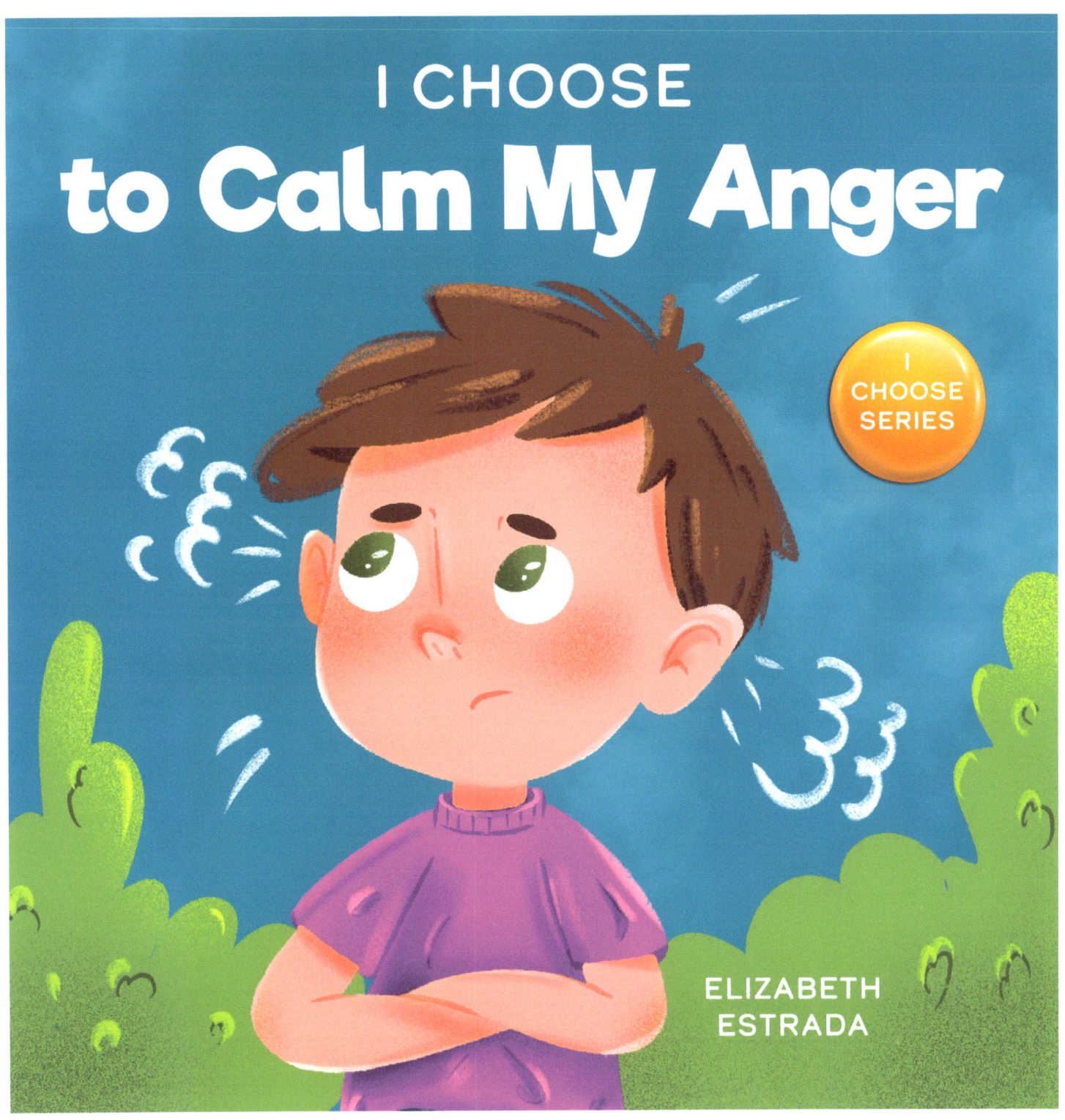

Today I feel...

_____

Draw a face showing the way you feel today.

Coping Skills

Coping skills teach you how to manage your emotions in a healthy manner.
Let's look at what are different ways to manage our feelings

Not so ideal	Ideal
Calling others names or saying bad words	Positive self talk and affirmations
Agressive behavior	Deep breaths
Hurting yourself or others	Doing something you love
Threatening	Exercising
Avoiding family and friends	Taking a time out
Screaming	Going for a walk
Blaming others	Talking it out

Trying something Different

Try responding differently when you're triggered.
Was the outcome a positive one?

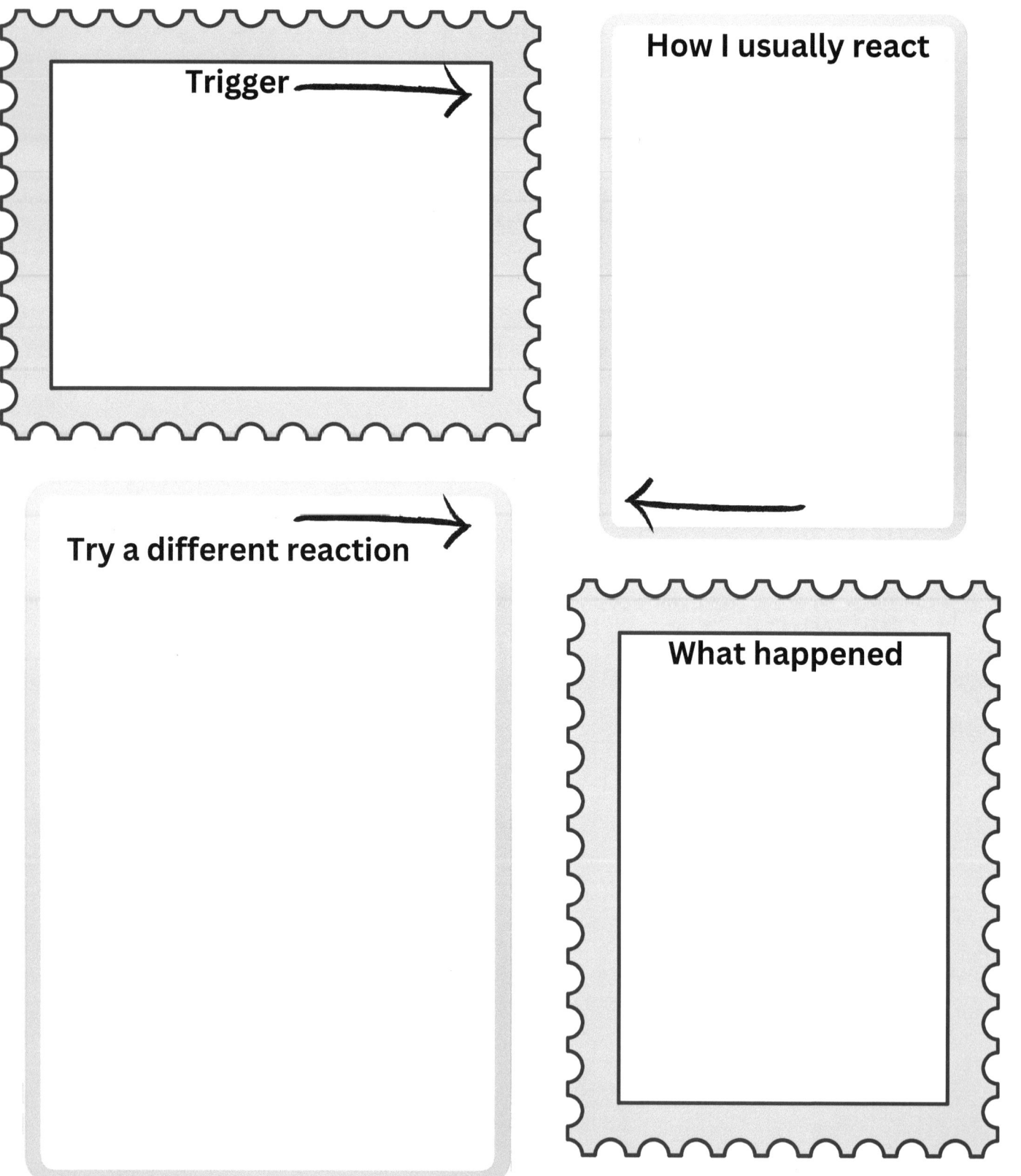

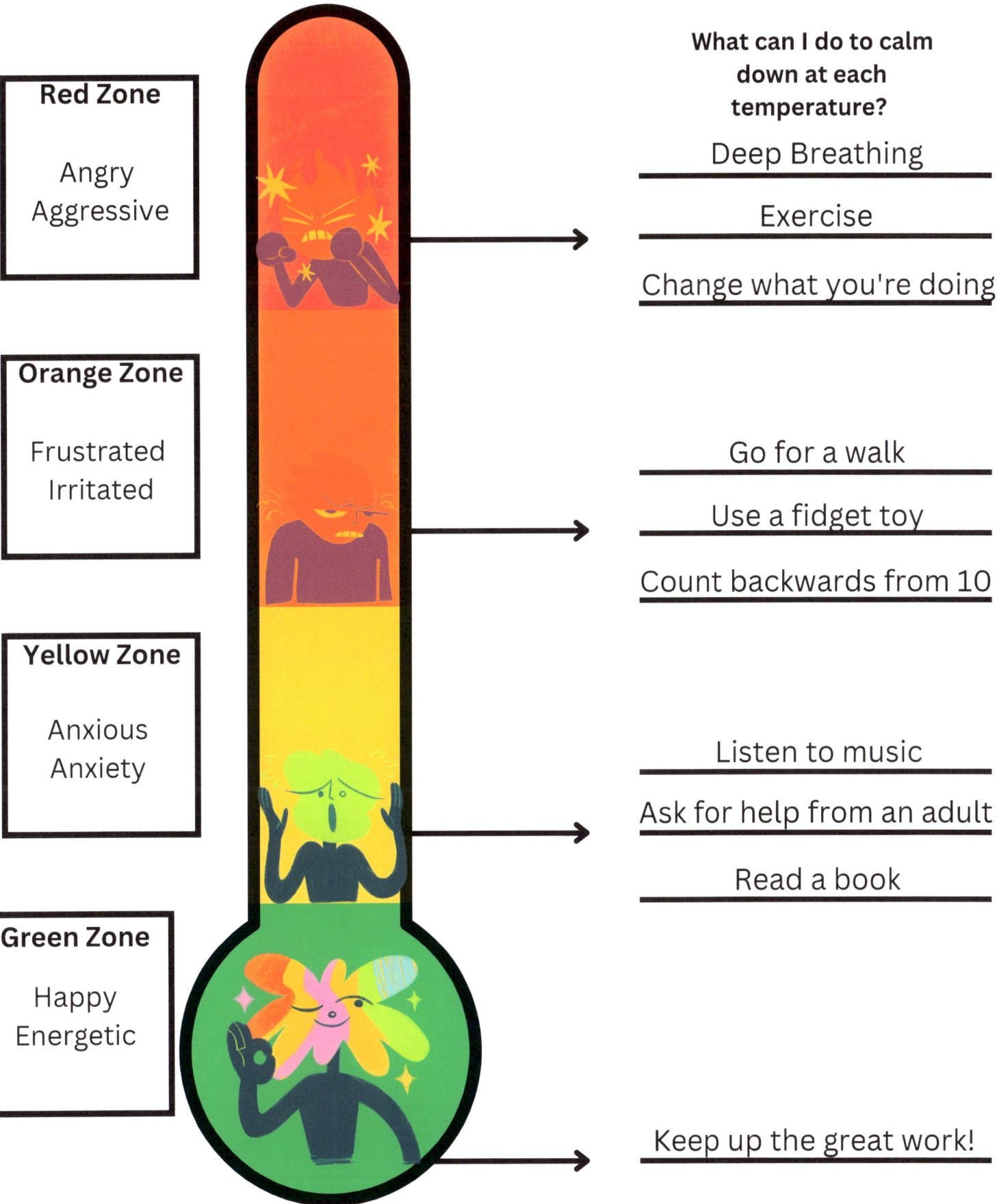

Circle of control

Brainstorm some things that you have no control of and then what you do have control of.

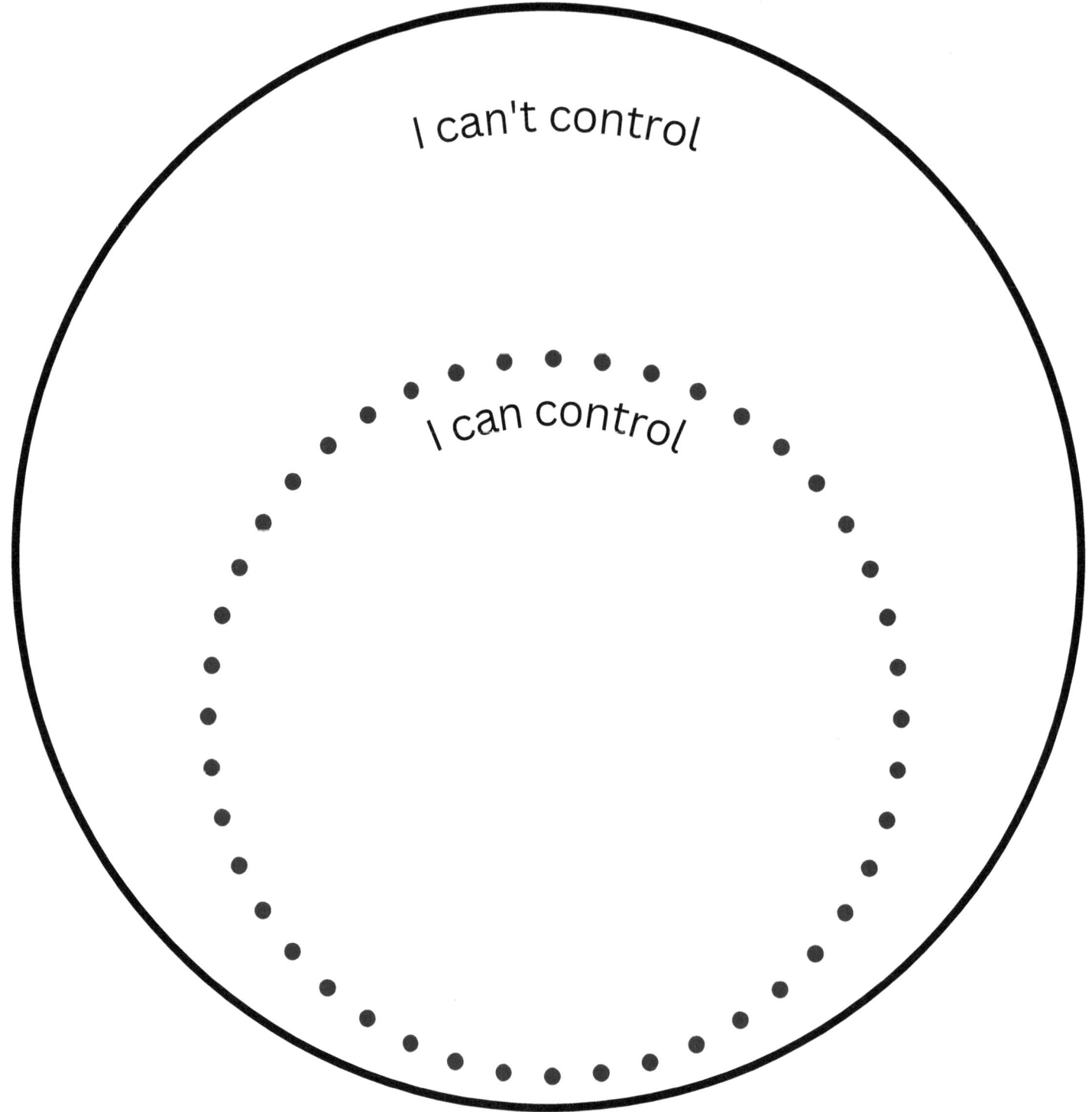

Here's some ideas

Other's opinions	What others say	Who my friends are	Effort I put in
The weather	What I say	Others actions	Being honest

Feeling Angry

Anger looks different for everyone.

- What does your face look like when you're angry? Draw it

- Write and draw 4 things that make you feel angry.

_____

_____

_____

_____

- Write and draw 4 ways in which you express that you are angry.

_____

_____

_____

_____

Socioemotional

TODAY I FEEL...

Color the jars according to how you feel today.

HAPPY

ANXIOUS

FUNNY

SURPRISED

ANGRY

Name:

Date:

Reflection Sheet

Here I can think about my anger and work towards solutions.

What triggered my anger?

Color how angry you feel from 1-5

Did I do or say anything I regret when I was angry?

Yes   No

Good job! It seems like you are using your coping skills and strategies effectively!

How did I act or behave when I was angry?

What can I do better next time?

Match the mood

Can you tell which color each face is expressing based from the mood themometer

Things That Make Me Angry
& THINGS THAT MAKE ME CALM
Write in the red clouds things that make you feel angry, and write in the blue clouds your favorite calming strategies.

ANGER ICEBERG

EXPLORING BELOW THE SURFACE

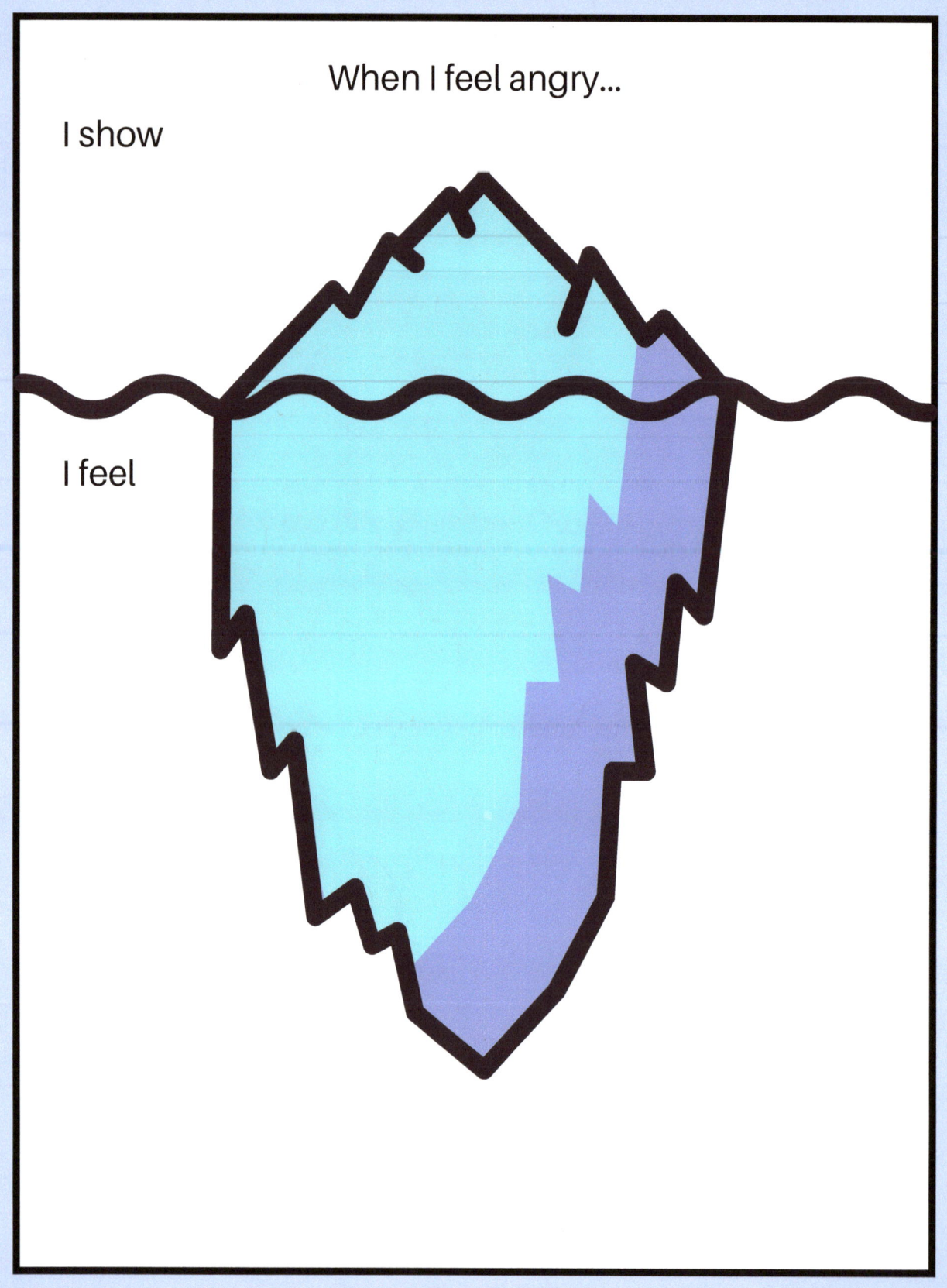

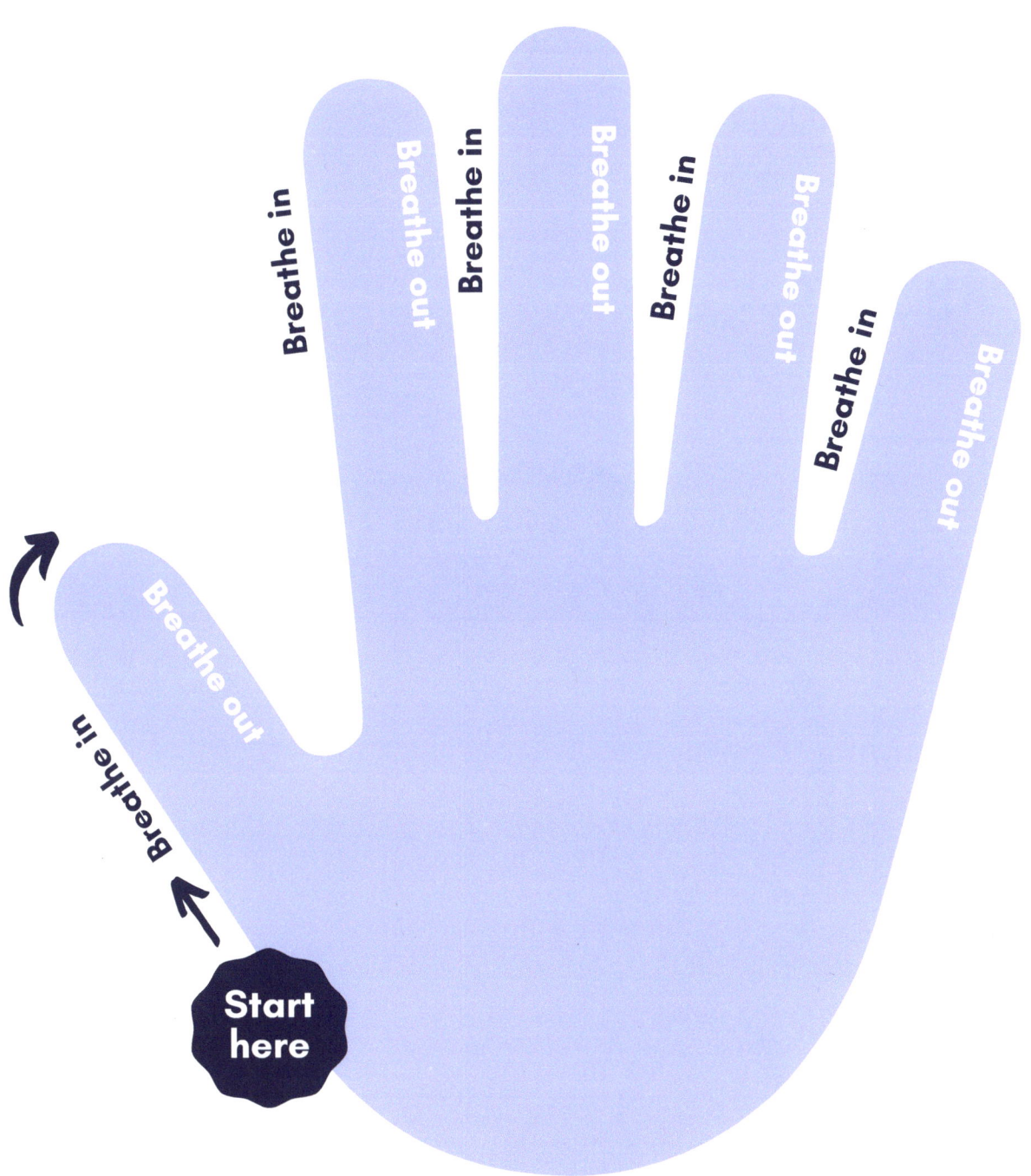

Today I feel...

Circle the way you feel.

Happy Sad Angry Nervous Excited

Tired Worried Focused Confused Joyful

Confident Upset

Write a word to describe your feelings.

Today I am...

_____

Draw a face showing the way you feel today..

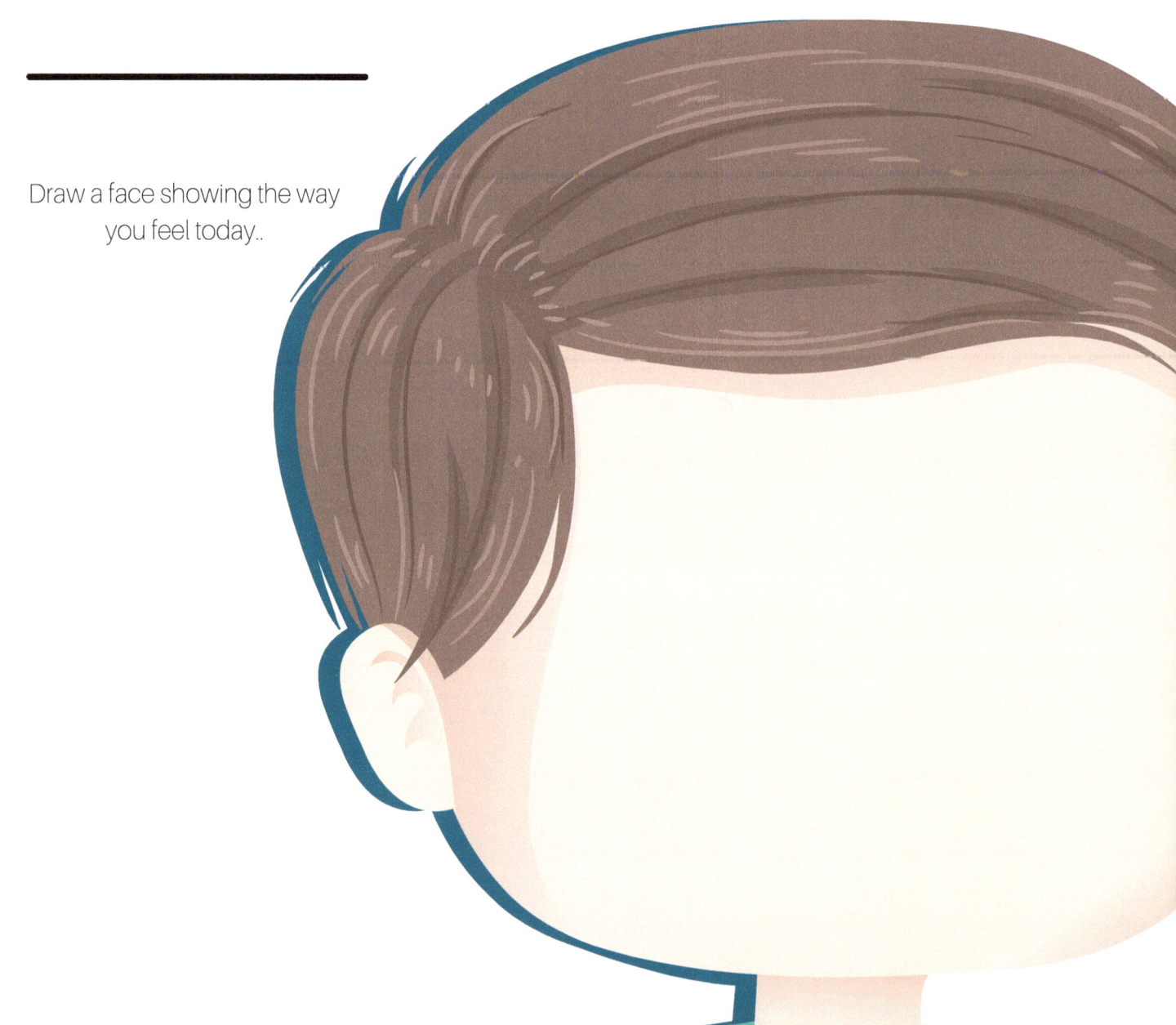

I Choose to Try Again
Lesson Plans

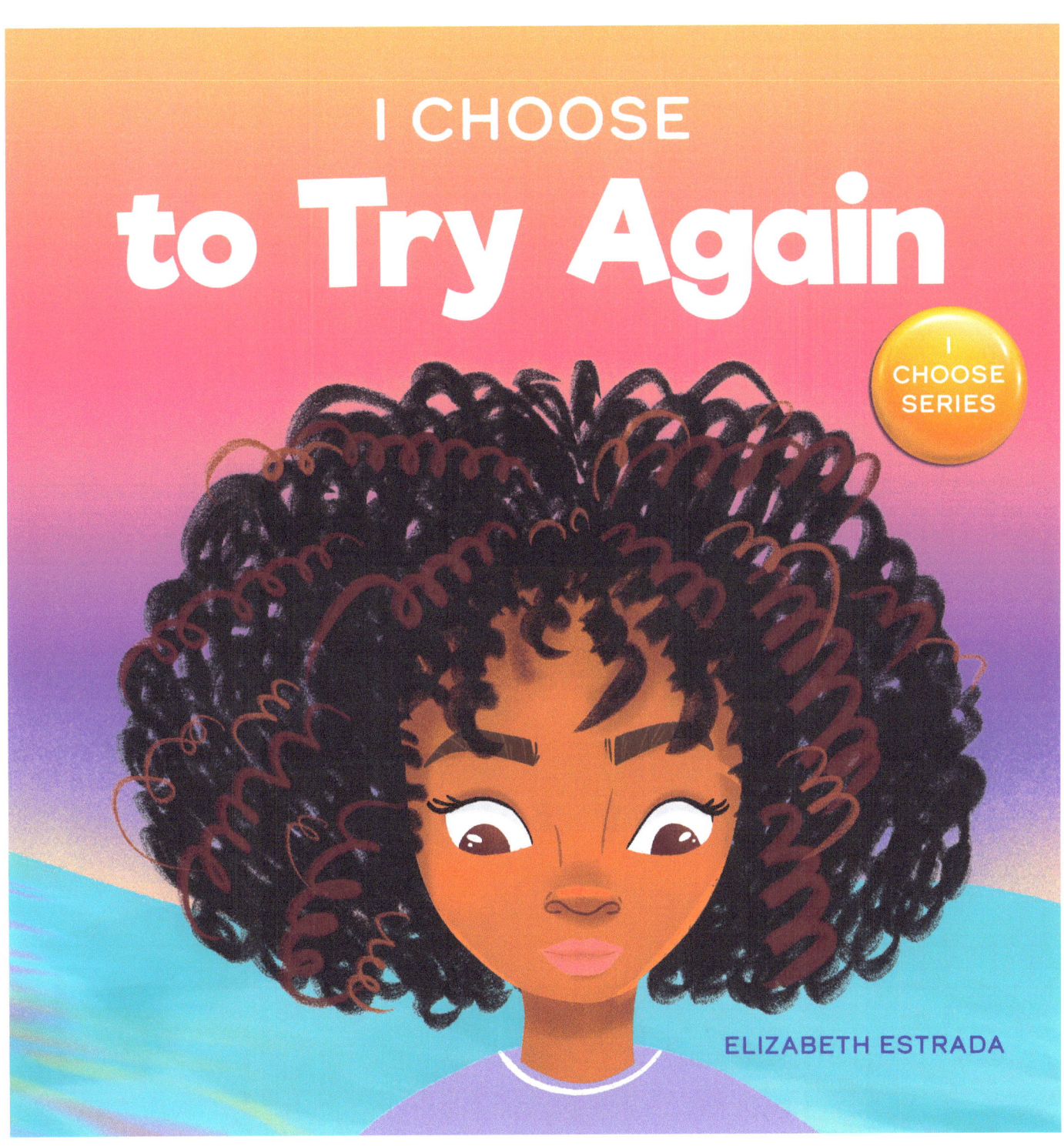

Name: _____ Date: _____

I MADE A MISTAKE

Which of the following can I do when I make a mistake?

- ☐ Be honest that I've made a mistake.
- ☐ Sincerely apologize to anyone affected.
- ☐ Forgive myself for making a mistake.
- ☐ Think of ways to do it better next time.
- ☐ Remind myself that everyone makes mistakes.
- ☐ Breathe, relax, and try again.
- ☐ Reflect on the mistake.
- ☐ Learn from my mistake.
- ☐ Address the root cause of my mistake.
- ☐ Share what I've learned.
- ☐ Allow myself to feel my emotions.
- ☐ Be patient with myself.
- ☐ Ask for help.
- ☐ Avoid the urge to dwell on the mistake.
- ☐ Remember that I am not a mistake.

Name: _____   Date: _____

SELF-FORGIVENESS

What was your mistake?

What emotions does this mistake make you feel?

What needs to be done for you to forgive yourself?

What have your learned?

What can you do differently next time if this situation happens again?

OVERCOMING MIND TRAPS

Name: _____   **Class:** _____

Looking at the 'mind traps' suggest mental reframes you could use to try to overcome them. Add more than one if you can think of a few!

'MIND TRAP' EXAMPLE	MENTAL REFRAME
I got that question wrong, I'm not smart!	I tried my best and I can try again next time.
It was just good luck that I scored that goal.	
It's out of my control.	
I can't do it.	
I'm always wrong.	
I'm not going to like it.	
I never get invited to things.	
Maths is just too hard for me.	
I'm never going to get better at this.	
I don't want to learn that.	

I AM WORTHY

COPING TOOLS
WHAT HELPS ME

- ☐ Take slow, mindful breaths
- ☐ Drink a warm cup of water
- ☐ Rest and take a break
- ☐ Stretch
- ☐ Journal or write a letter
- ☐ Listen to your favorite music
- ☐ Talk to someone you trust
- ☐ Get a hug
- ☐ Cuddle or play with your pet
- ☐ Use positive affirmations
- ☐ Use a stress ball
- ☐ Blow bubbles
- ☐ Make an artwork
- ☐ Hug or climb a tree
- ☐ Read a book or magazine
- ☐ Take a shower or bath

Name: _____   Date: _____

SOCIAL EMOTIONAL
TIC-TAC-TOE

Do the activity in the middle and then choose two more activities in a row (vertically, horizontally or diagonally) to complete the Tic-Tac-Toe

Write your top 3 wishes and find a place to keep them	Perform a random act of kindness in your class today	Draw a poster of something you want to change in the world
Practice mindful breathing for 5 minutes	Write or draw 5 things you are grateful for	Draw a picture of a time when you helped someone
Show how you feel right now, by drawing an abstract picture.	Write a list of what you love most about yourself	Write a thank you note to someone who has changed your life

CONTROLLED *breathing*

Starting on the dot, follow the breathing prompts while you trace your finger around the star in a clockwise direction.

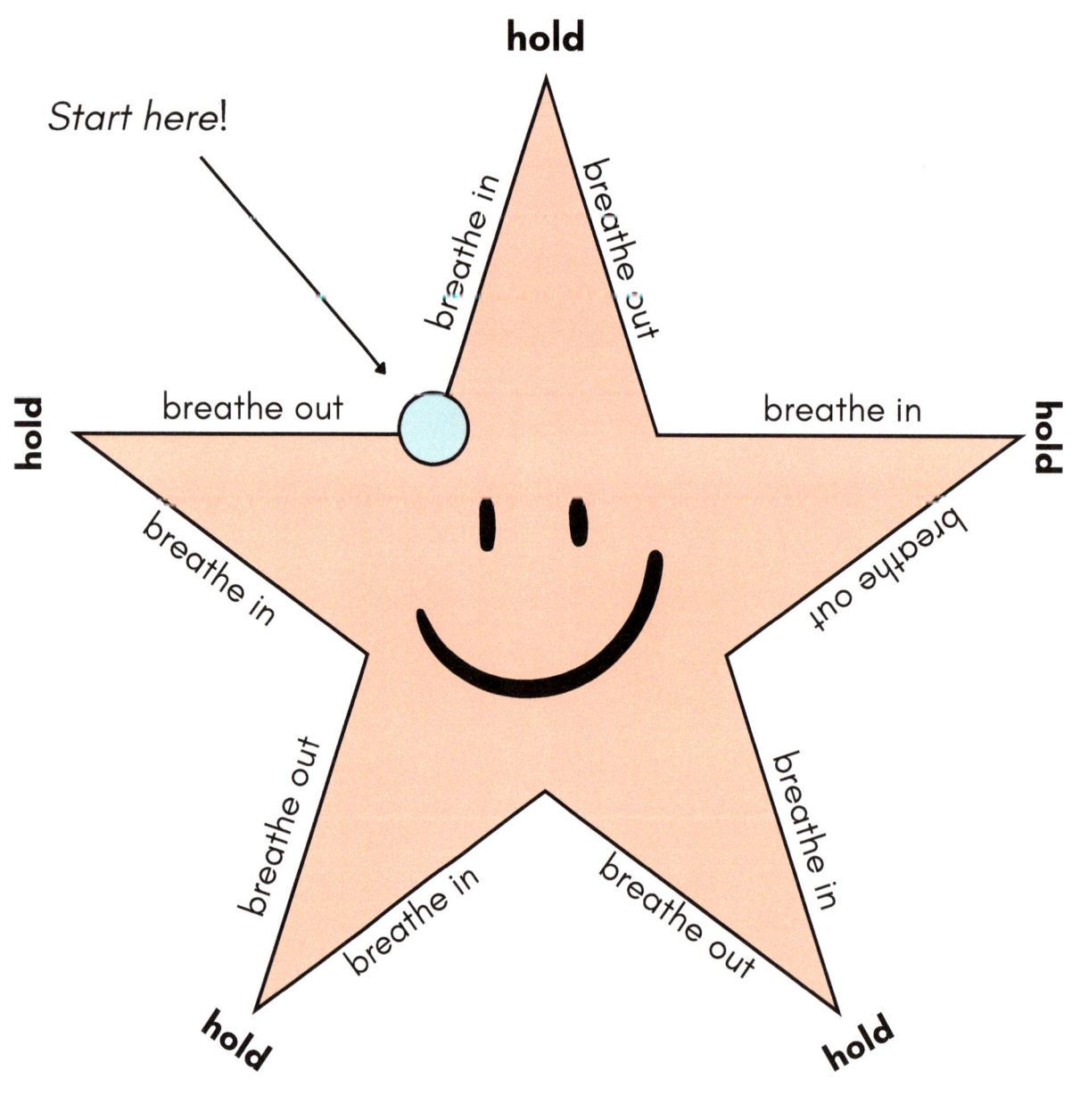

Name _____ Date _____

RELEASE YOUR WORRIES

Imagine a tree that absorbs your worries when you hug it. Draw or write down your worries on the tree. Then talk about them with someone who cares about you.

GOAL WORKSHEET

DATE:

GOAL:

WHY?

STEPS TO TAKE

- --
- --
- --
- --

NOTES

Name: Class:

Check-in

Feelings can be overwhelming for us and that is completely okay! Check-in with your own feelings and see if you can figure them out. Then, fill this container with feeling colors to show how much of each you have right now.

| Angry = Red | Happy = Yellow | Sad = Blue |
| Nervous = Purple | Excited = Green | Calm = Orange |

CHIT CHAT CUBE

Use a conversation starters in small and large group settings.

	What is your favorite thing about yourself?	
Talk about a time you made someone proud.	What is the best present you have ever received?	Talk about your pet, or a pet you wish you could have.
	What is your favorite memory?	
	Who is the nicest person you know, and why?	

I Choose Kindness
Lesson Plans

Cut Out Hearts

Cut out all of the yellow hearts below and place in a jar that you have or a small box. Each day try to do something kind by practicing the heart you grab from the jar each day.

Ways You Can Show Kindness

- Take a few breaths before answering someone
- Make a kind gesture
- Smile
- Write a kind note
- Hold the door for someone
- Give a compliment
- Sing a song to a friend
- Pick up your toys

Ways You Can Show Kindness

- Give a hug to a family member
- Ask your mom or dad if they need help with anything
- Open the door for someone else
- Call a family member just to say hi
- Help a friend in need
- Tell someone else what makes them special
- Pick a flower and give it to someone
- Pick up trash

Kindness Cards

Give out kindness card to make someone smile today!

Name:_____

Kindness is
GOLDEN

Directions: Fill the pot of gold with names of people that you can show kindness to. Write about ways you can show kindness on the pot and color in the picture.

Creative Thinking Task

TASK:

Create a new label for a can of food. Fill it with something that money cannot buy. Some ideas could include: kindness, silence or a smile.

Creative Thinking Task

TASK:

Create a new label for a can of food. Fill it with something that money cannot buy. Some ideas could include: kindness, silence or a smile.

CONVERSATION CARDS

- How many brothers or sisters do you have?
- What do you do on Sundays?
- When do you usually do your homework?
- Where do you go shopping?
- How often do you eat fast food?
- Who is the strongest person in your family?
- Talk about a calm animal. How do you know it is calm?
- What do you usually do in the evening?
- How do birds keep their babies safe?

Name: _____ Date: _____

5 Ways to Be Kind

1. _____
   _____

2. _____
   _____

3. _____
   _____

4. _____
   _____

5. _____
   _____

Kindness is…

_____

_____

I Choose to Calm My Anxiety
Lesson Plans

Letting Go

Write what you can control in the blue balloons and what you can't in the red balloons and let go of the worries that are out of your control. Imagine them floating away just like these balloons.

Name: _____ Date: _____

MY WORRY JAR

A worry jar is a useful tool that can help you express your worries and anxious thoughts. What are some things that make you feel worried? Write them in the jar below.

Think of a special time each day when you will open your worry jar and read your worries. You can do this with someone you trust.

What time will you open your worry jar?

Who is going to be with you?

Name _____ Date _____

LETTING GO OF MY THOUGHTS

What are some anxious thoughts that you might need to let go? Write them on the balloons below. Then talk about these thoughts with someone who cares about you.

Feeling Worried

Worry looks different for everyone.

- What does your face look like when you're worried? Draw it

- Write and draw 4 things that make you feel worried.

_____
_____
_____
_____

- Write and draw 4 ways in which you express that you are worried.

_____
_____
_____
_____

Five Senses

When you feel anxious remember the five senses to calm your anxiety.

Step 1: Look for five things you can see

Step 2: Touch four things that are near you

Step 3: Listen for three thing you can hear

Step 4: Smell two things that are near you

Step 5: Taste one thing

Name: _____ Date: _____

ANXIETY BREAKDOWN

What is making you feel anxious?

What thoughts are going through your head?

How is your body responding?

What is the worst thing that can happen?

What can you control in this situation?

What can you do to calm your body?

name: _____   class: _____

3-2-1 Reflection

3 Things I Learned 💡

1. _____
2. _____
3. _____

2 Things I Found Interesting

1. _____
2. _____

1 Question I Still Have ❓

1. _____

Mindfulness Coloring

I Choose to Reduce, Reuse, Recycle
Lesson Plans

everyday is EARTH DAY

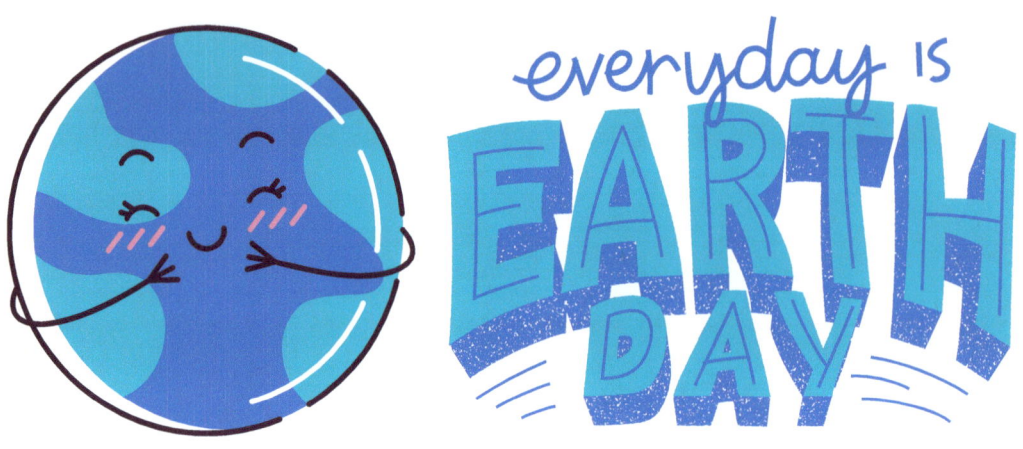

What can you do to protect Earth every day? Draw and write

EARTH DAY

Fun Activity Book

Name:

SORT AND RECYCLE

Draw a line from the object to the correct recycle bin.

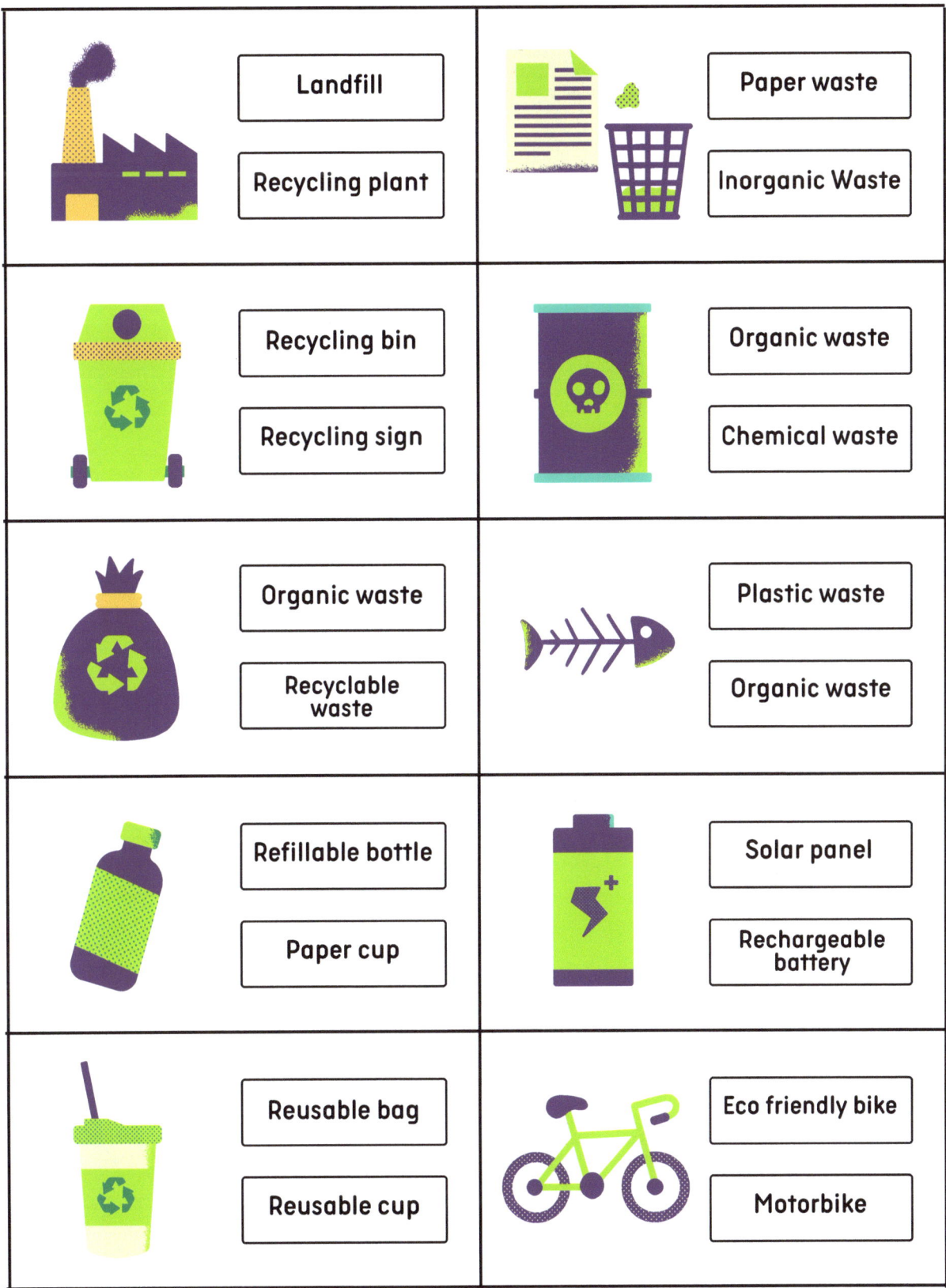

Name: _____ Date: _____

RECYCLING

Draw or write examples of litter for each of the categories:

Dot to Dot

Follow the numbers to connect each dot.

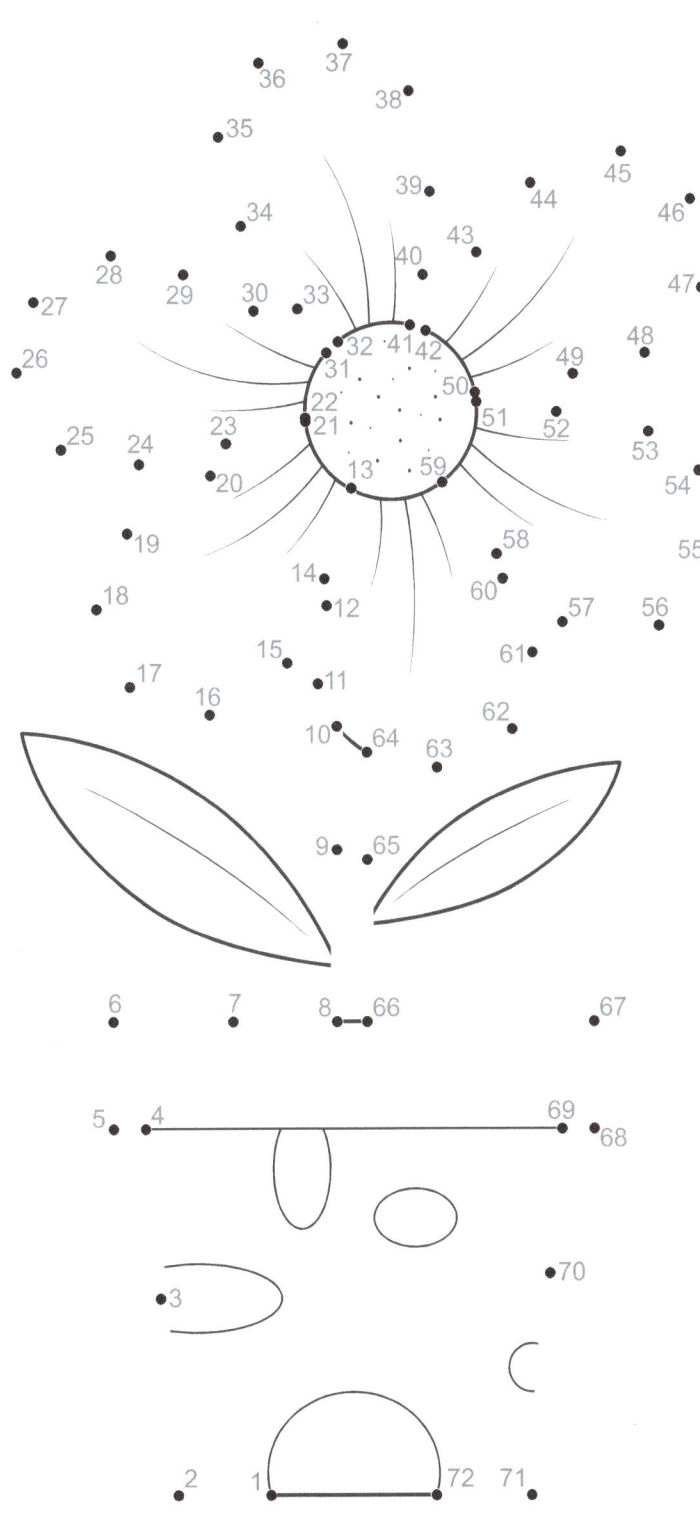

EARTH DAY WASTE SORTING

Draw a line from the waste groups to the correct bins.

FIND THE WORDS
EARTH DAY

Write the words under the pictures.

| plastic bag | recycle | water | reusable bag |
| plastic bottle | flower | sprout | organic waste |

_____

_____

Name: _____ Date: _____

WASTE SORTING

Color the waste with the color corresponding to the recycling bin.

Maze Madness

Help the sea turtle finish each maze!

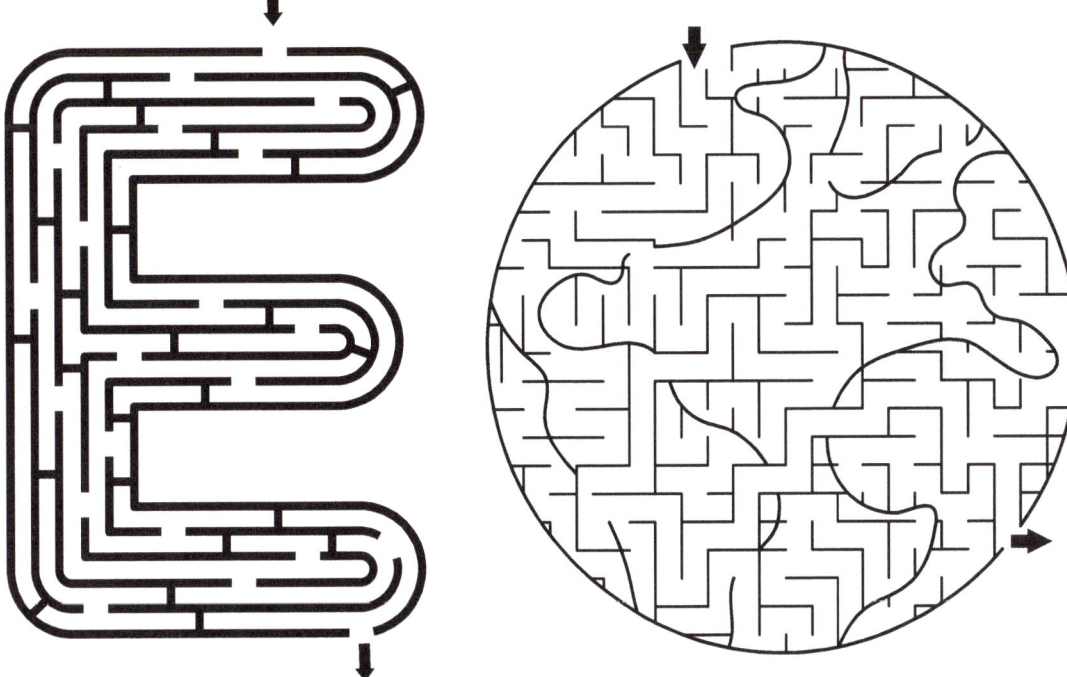

Student: _____

E-WASTE

Circle pictures that need to be thrown into the container for e-waste.

Earth Day Scissors Skills

Carefully practice your scissors skill by cutting from the bottom to the recycled items.

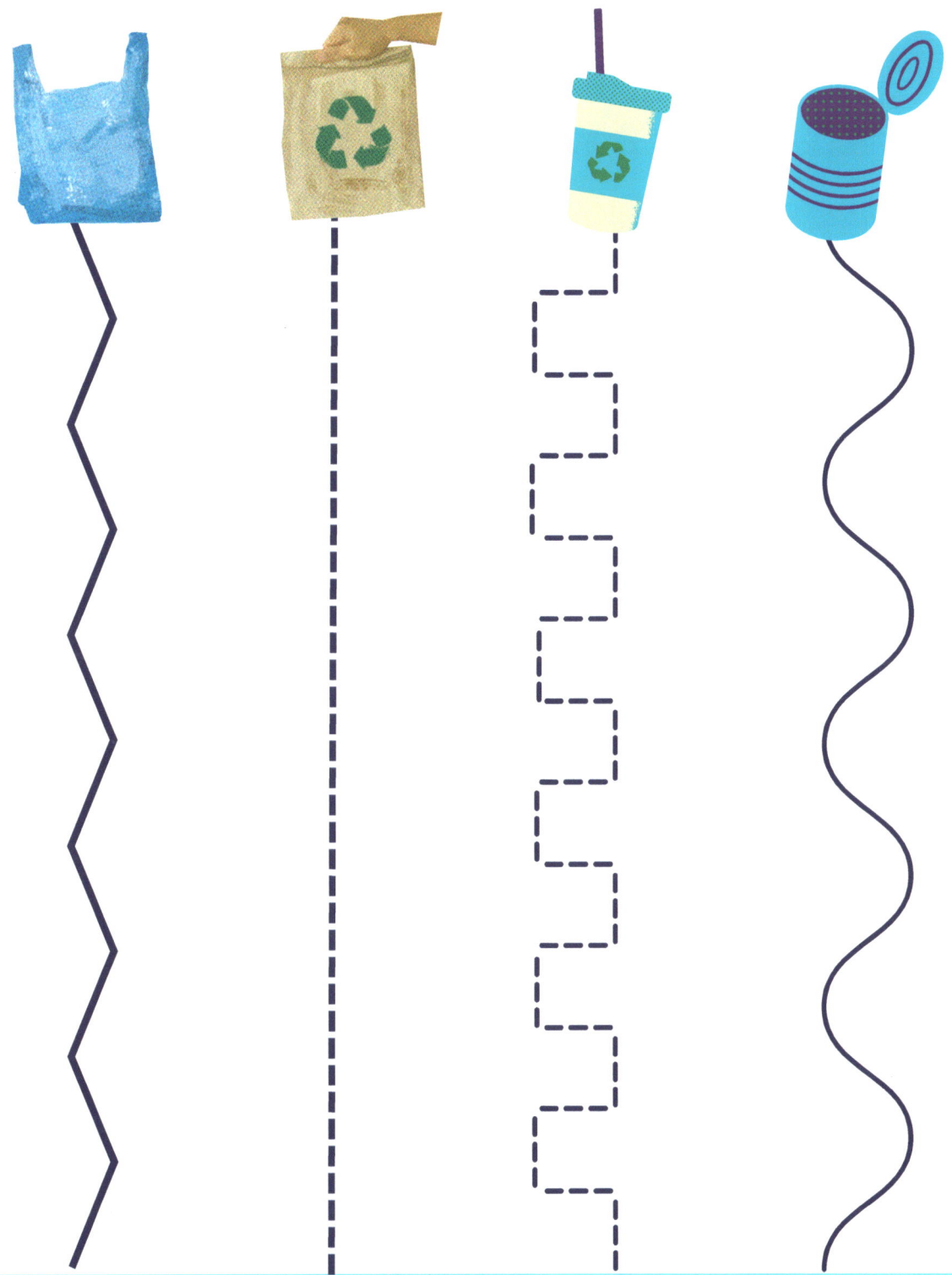

Fruits Lacing Cards

Print, cut out and laminate the picture. Use a hole puncher to punch all the holes. You can practice lacing the picture by using a shoelace or wool.

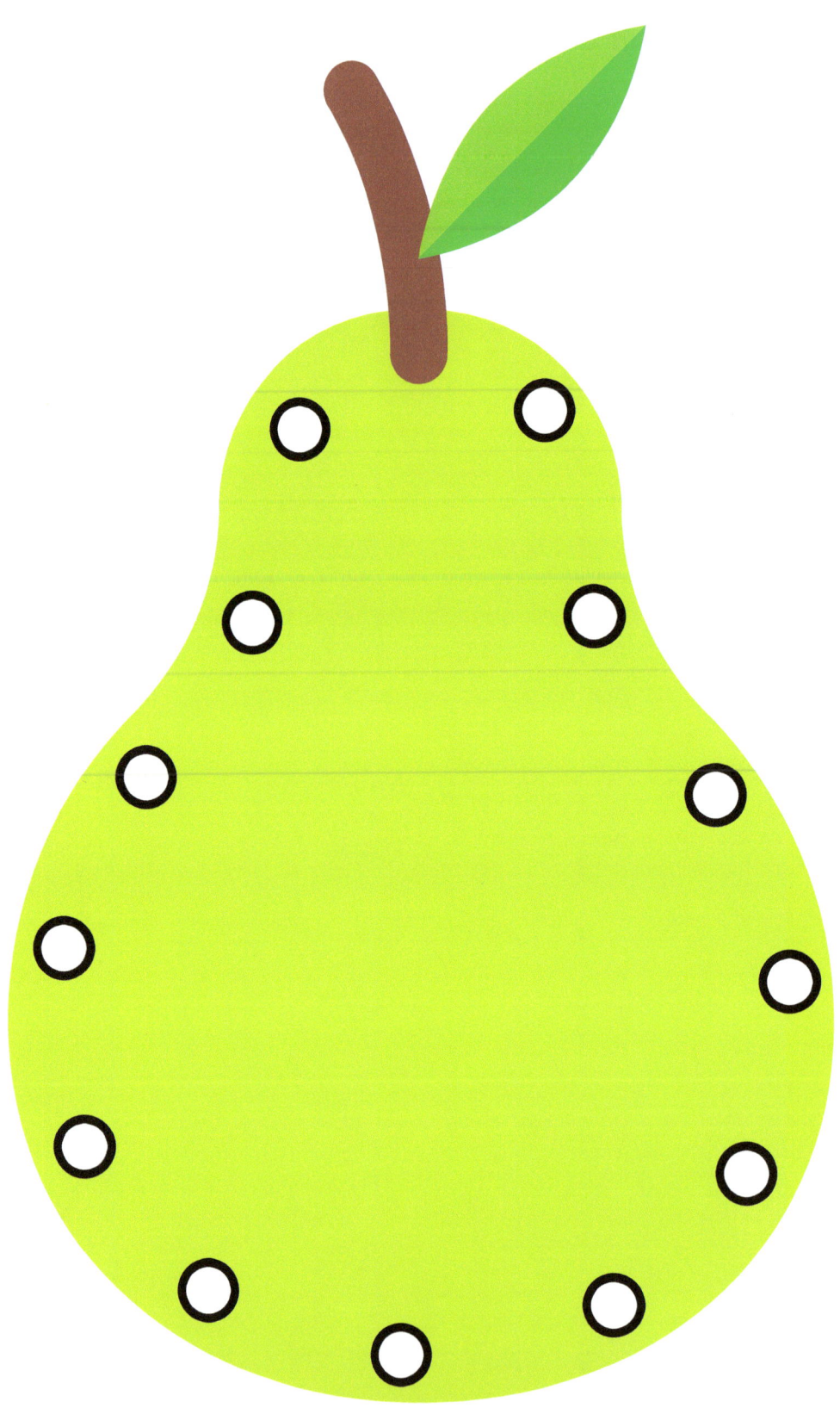

Name: _____

What's the weather?

Direction: Match the weather and the words.

   •   • sunny

   •   • cloudy

   •   • stormy

   •   • snowy

   •   • rainy

   •   • windy

EARTH DAY

APRIL 22

What can you do to protect Earth?
Draw and write

I can save

_____

_____

I can reduce

_____

_____

I can reuse

_____

_____

I can recycle

_____

_____

EARTH DAY
22ND APRIL 2022

NAME: _____   CLASS: _____

What is the purpose of Earth Day?

State 3 things we can do to support looking after Earth:

Find 3 organisations that contribute to caring for the planet:

Share 3 reasons you believe it is important to care for the earth:

EARTH DAY
REFERENCES
Note the websites you used to find your information.

1.
2.
3.
4.
5.
6.

Sort out the following actions. Which ones are good and which ones are bad for the environment?

| reuse bags   cut down trees   waste water   pollute the air   recycle
plant trees   turn off the lights   use lots of plastic bags   drop litter
leave the lights on   walk or ride a bike   protect animals |

Good for the environment	Bad for the environment
....	....
....	....
....	....
....	....
....	....

Name: _____   Date: _____

EARTH
TIC-TAC-TOE

Do the activity in the middle and then choose two more activities in a row (vertically, horizontally or diagonally) to complete the Tic-Tac-Toe

Create a "Save the Earth" slogan and design a poster using it	Create an Earth guardian hero and make a comic strip about him	Write a paragraph describing what you can do to protect the Earth
Write and illustrate the instructions to reuse a plastic container	**Create a song, a rap or a poem about the 3Rs**	Write a list of Earth's natural resources and share it with your class
Draw the Earth and write a fact file with its main characteristics as a planet	Compare and contrast planet Earth with another planet, using a Venn diagram	Watch a video or read a book about planet Earth and share a fact that you have learnt from it

I Choose Happy
Lesson Plans

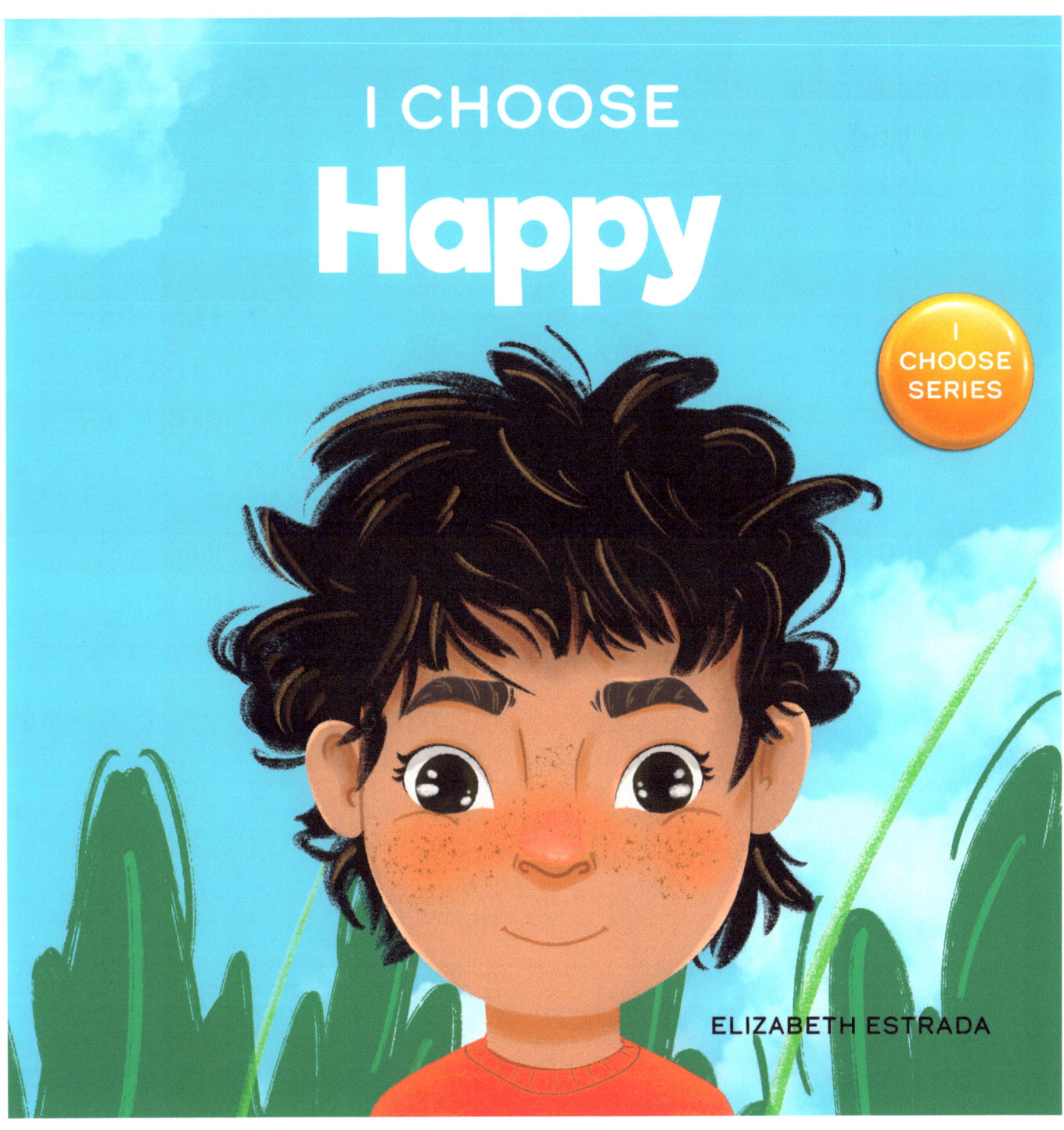

Things I can do when I'm feeling strong emotions

1. I can exercise my body
2. I can ask to step out
3. I can listen to relaxing music
4. Splash cold water on my face
5. Use positive talk and give myself affirmations
6. I can take a walk
7. Use deep breathing exercises
8. Write in my diary
9. Go for a swim
10. Read a good book

Right now I feel...

Fill in the monitor(s) to show how you feel today

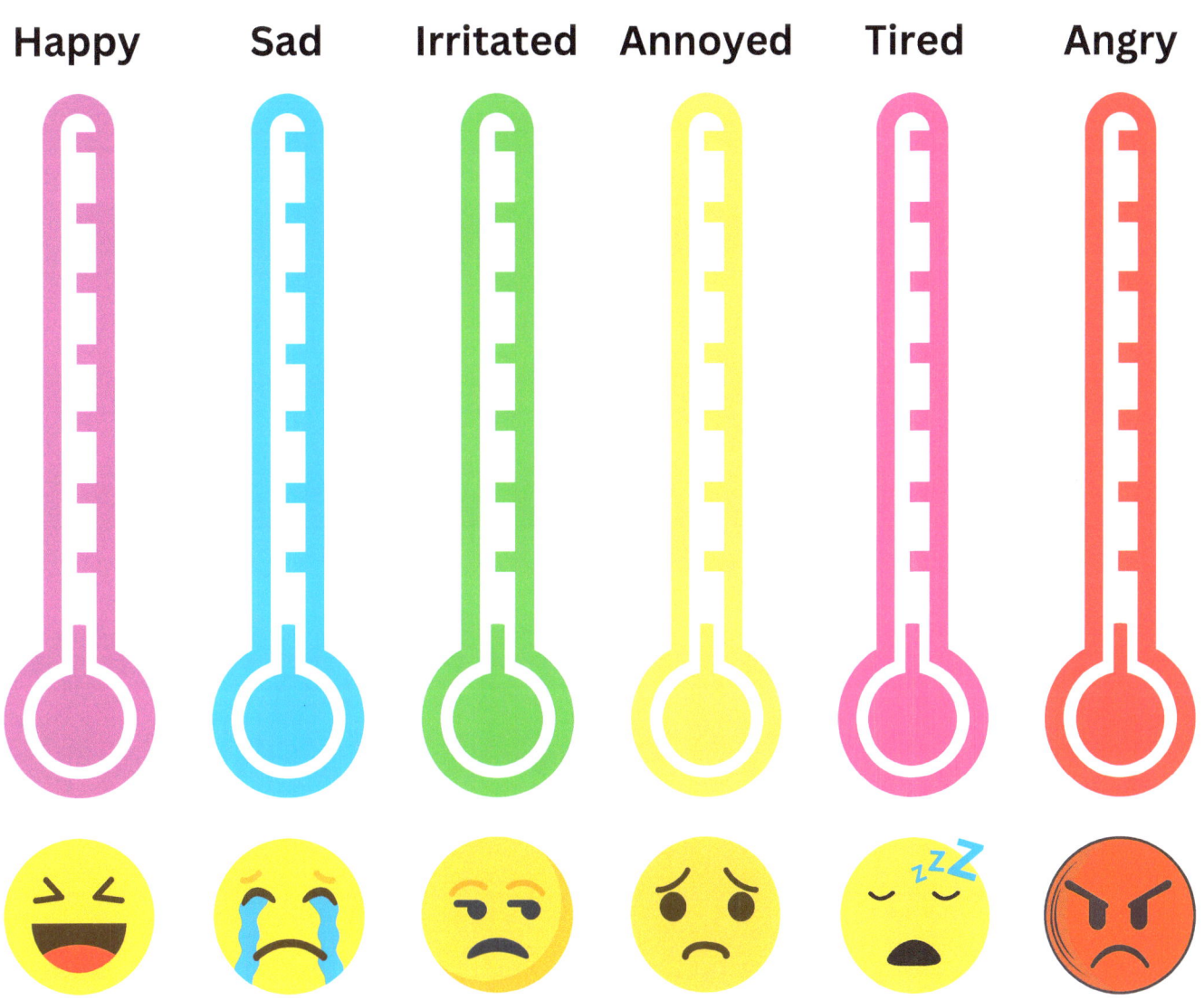

Example

Create your very own feelings cake!

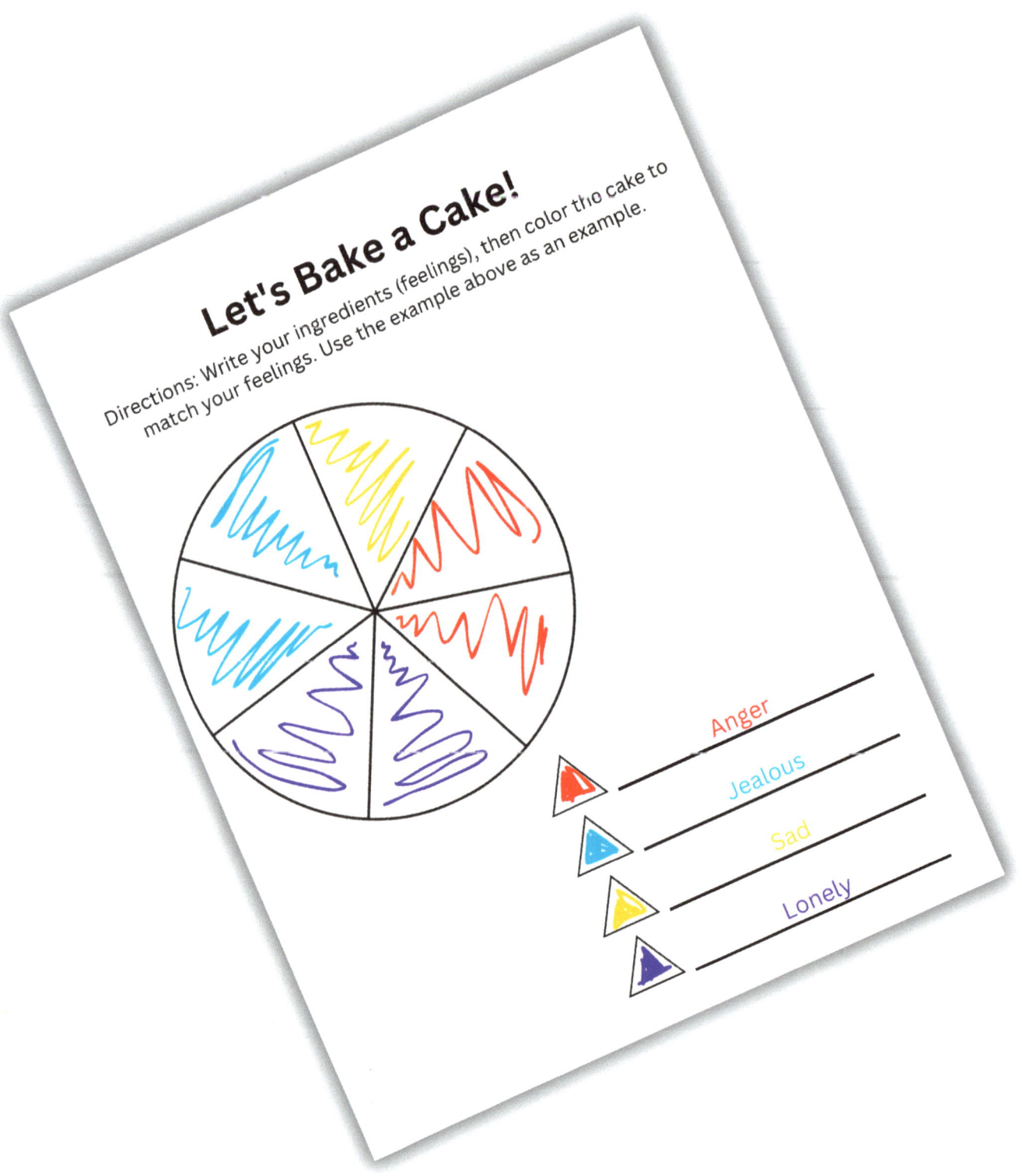

Let's Bake a Cake!

Directions: Write your ingredients (feelings), then color the cake to match your feelings. Use the example above as an example.

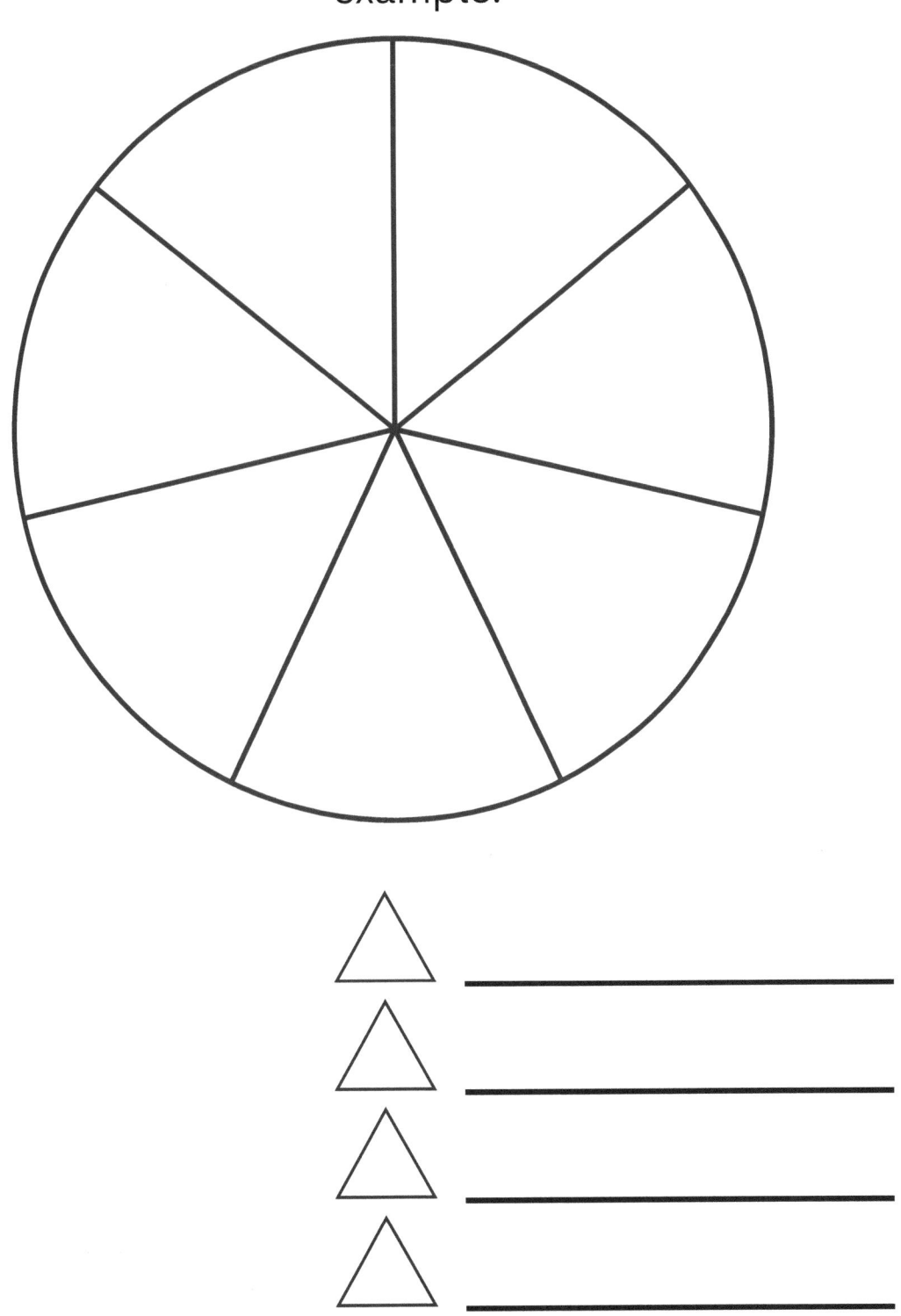

Name _____   Date _____

MY DAILY JOURNAL

I felt   The weather was

The three things I am grateful for today are

-
-
-

The best thing about today

Today I learned   Today I helped

Feeling Happy

Happiness looks different for everyone.

- What does your face look like when you're happy? Draw it

- Write and draw 4 things that make you feel happy.

_____

_____

_____

_____

- Write and draw 4 ways in which you express that you are happy.

_____

_____

_____

_____

Name _____ Date _____

MY FEELINGS

Feelings are physical sensations you feel in your body. How does it feel in your body when you are feeling...

FEELINGS
WORD SCRAMBLE

Unscramble the words below

mlac

Calm

riprussed

Surprised

ticexde

Excited

elsepy

Sleepy

deriorw

Worried

dsa

Sad

yphap

Happy

reacsd

Scared

grany

Angry

edirt

Tired

Name: _____

Feelings

Can you tell how each kid feel?
Circle the correct answer.

	sick happy sleepy
	angry sleepy sick
	fine sad sick
	happy sick sleepy
	angry sad fine
	sad angry happy

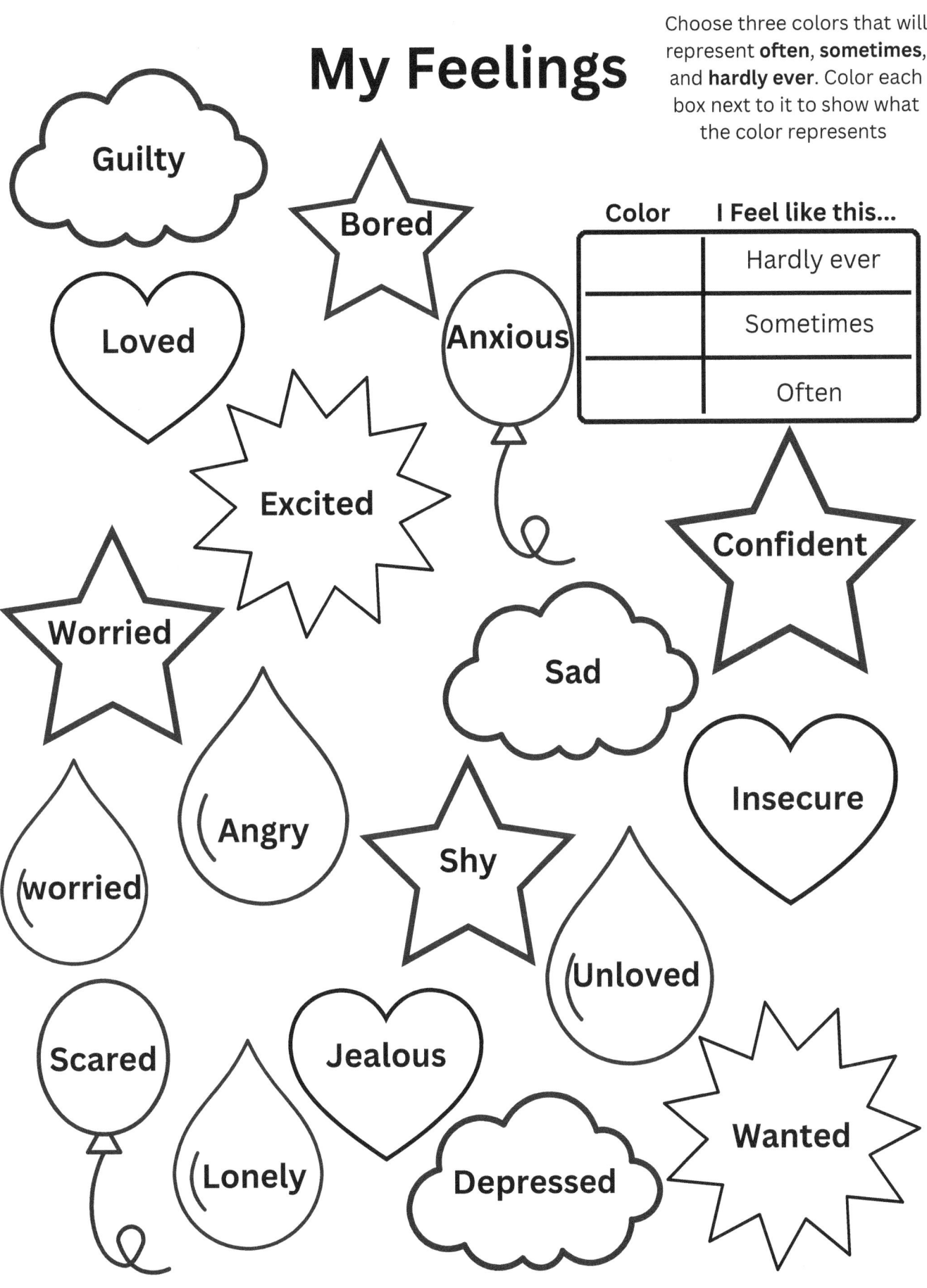

www.ingramcontent.com/pod-product-compliance
Lightning Source LLC
Chambersburg PA
CBHW041103070526
44583CB00002B/35